CW01429076

CROSS-CULTURAL DISCIPLESHIP
MAKING GOD'S NAME KNOWN IN EVERY NATION

REFUGIO
MINISTRIES

Contents

introduction   4

1.1   6

Heart of the disciple: identity in christ   6

1.2   9

biblical theology   9

1.3   16

Case study: biblical theology   16

2.1   17

heart of the disciple: fear   17

2.2   20

cultural differences   20

2.3   30

Cultural values defined   30

3.1   32

heart of the disciple: Humility   32

3.2   35

contextualization   35

3.3   44

case study: To catch a thief   44

4.1   46

heart of the disciple: forgiveness   46

4.2   49

culture shock   49

4.3   56

case study: culture shock   56

5.1   58

heart of disciple: dependence on the holy spirit 58

5.2   62

church planting   62

5.3   69

The missionary church   69

conclusion   70

about Refugio ministries   71

bibliography   73

INTRODUCTION

Cross-cultural discipleship is an urgent calling to make God known among all the peoples of the earth. Jesus looked over the people with compassion and appealed to his disciples, "The harvest is plentiful, but the laborers are few; therefore pray earnestly to the Lord of the harvest to send out laborers into his harvest" (ESV, Luke 9:37-38)[1].

Following Jesus and making disciples requires sacrifice, perseverance, training, and preparation. The enemy recognizes the threat of disciple makers and will attack their identity, strike fear into them, distract them with pride and selfish gain, cause them to resent others, and allow them to be distracted with ministry while they neglect their dependence on the Holy Spirit. God is not as interested in what you do but who you are and how you are being transformed. The enemy distracts missionaries and ministry leaders with ministry strategy and tasks so that they forget their identity in Christ and their need for the Holy Spirit.

The purpose of this book is to provide a brief introduction to those interested in cross-cultural discipleship and to examine the heart of the disciple. Each chapter is divided into three sections. The first section examines the heart of the disciple. This has been adapted from Receiving His Life Ministries.

---

[1] Unless otherwise noted, all biblical passages referenced are in the *English Standard Version* (Wheaton, IL: Crossway, 2008).

The second section of each chapter analyzes various elements of cross-cultural ministry. First, the importance of Biblical theology will be analyzed. Next cultural differences will be examined, then the importance of contextualization, culture shock, and church planting will be assessed.

The final section concludes the chapter with a case study. Finally, the book concludes with next steps for those interested in pursuing cross-cultural discipleship or supporting cross-cultural workers. Cross-cultural discipleship requires Biblical preparation and study and, most importantly, examination of the heart.

1.1

HEART OF THE DISCIPLE: IDENTITY IN CHRIST

The moment one places their faith in Christ, they are born again and have access to the abundant life and freedom promised by Jesus. Many believers do not experience complete freedom and abundant life as the enemy comes to kill, steal and destroy (John 10:10). Maturing believers and ministry leaders often fall back into slavery as Satan is the father of lies (John 8:44) and will try to deceive believers.

The enemy may be saying you are not qualified to disciple and lead others, you may be experiencing guilt and shame from previous or ongoing sin and addiction, and he may be accusing you of being a fraud. You are not alone, as believers are called to suffer with Christ in the power of the Holy Spirit. You are going to stumble daily, but you have been made a perfect child of God through Jesus and the Holy Spirit living in you.

I. You have a new identity in Christ.

John 3:3-8 (believers are born again of the Spirit), 2 Cor. 5:17-21 (believers are a new creation), **Gal. 5:24-25 (the flesh has been**

crucified and believers live by the Spirit), Eph. 5:20-24 (Put off your old self), Col. 1:21-22 (Believers are reconciled by the death of Jesus), Ez. 36:26-27 (God will give us a new heart and new spirit).

Meditate on Gal. 5:24-25

1. What passions and desires continue to have a hold on you?

2. How do you keep in step with the Spirit?

3. What causes ministry leaders to become conceited and envious?

II. Believers are children of God and loved by God.

John 1:12-13 (children of God), **Rom. 8:12-17 (You did not receive a spirit of slavery in fear but a Spirit of adoption)**, John 17:23 (the Father loves the son as he does believers), John 3:16-17 (God loves the world), Rom. 9:6-8 (Believers are children of the promise)

Meditate on Rom. 8:12-17

1. What causes you to fear?

2. How do you relate to God as your Father?

3. How does it make you feel that you are to suffer with Christ in order to bc glorified in him?

III. Believers have been made righteous and free.

Rom. 5:19 (By one man's obedience believers were made righteous), Rom. 6:19 (Believers are slaves to righteousness and not to impurity), Rom. 6:6-14 (Believers are not enslaved to sin), John 8:34-36 (The Son sets believers free), 1 John 3:7-10 (No one

7

born of God can keep on sinning), 1 Cor. 15:55-57 (There is victory over death and sin through Jesus), John 16:33 (Jesus has overcome the world), **Gal. 5:1 (Christ has set us free)**

1. How are you experiencing freedom?

2. How do ministry leaders fall into a yoke of slavery?

IV. Believers have abundant life.

Rom. 8:11 (The Spirit gives life to our mortal bodies), John 6:57 (whoever feeds on Jesus will live), **John 10:10 (Jesus gives us abundant life), Matt. 11:28-30 (Jesus gives us rest)**, 1 Peter 5:6-7 (cast all your anxieties on Jesus)

Meditate on John 10:10

1.What is the enemy killing, stealing, and destroying in your life?

2.How are you living life abundantly?

V. Believers are forgiven.

Heb. 8:12 (God will not remember our sins), Ps. 103:1-3 (God forgives all our iniquity), John 3:16-17, **Ps. 32:1-2 (Our transgressions are forgiven)**

Meditate on Ps. 32:1-2

1. What do you need to confess to God or a trusted friend in order to experience full freedom?

2.What lies are you believing regarding your true identity in Christ?

1.2

BIBLICAL THEOLOGY

While important doctrinal beliefs are organized systematically in systematic theology, biblical theology ensures that those beliefs are biblical by interpreting them as a unified story of God centered around Jesus. Biblical theology articulates doctrinal beliefs as it considers the worldview of the author and interprets the original meaning of the biblical authors.

The Author's Worldview

The text should be understood in the context and culture in which the authors were writing Scripture. Scripture was inspired by the Holy Spirit, but it was revealed to the authors in a different culture and context than in the culture that it is being read today. James Hamilton refers to biblical theology as the interpretative perspective of the authors, which is the framework of assumptions and presuppositions of the author.[2] Biblical theology considers the worldview of the author as the authors have presumptions and assumptions. Peter explained,

---

[2] James M. Hamilton Jr, What is Biblical Theology? Wheaton: Crossway, 2014.

9

And we have the prophetic word more fully confirmed, to which you will do well to pay attention as to a lamp shining in a dark place, until the day dawns and the morning star rises in your hearts, knowing this first of all, that no prophesy of Scripture comes from someone's own interpretation. For no prophesy was ever produced by the will of man, but men spoke from God as they were being carried along by the Holy Spirit (2 Peter 1:19-21).

As Peter said, the Holy Spirit communicated the message to the prophets, but they were only human and understood and recorded the message according to their assumptions and beliefs. Biblical theology considers those beliefs within the context and culture in which they were living.

1. How can contemporary readers understand the worldview of the authors?

The Inspiration of Scripture

The biblical authors presumed the authority of their writings as the Word of God. Tim Chester and Steve Timmis noted, "God rules as his word is trusted and obeyed. God is rejected when his word is not trusted and obeyed."[3] Doctrinal beliefs should be grounded in Scripture, and Biblical theology confirms the authority of those beliefs are not taken out of context but agree with the remainder of Scripture as a whole. Paul wrote, "All scripture is given by

---

[3] Tim Chester and Steve Timmis, *Total Church*, Wheaton, IL: Crossway, 2008, p.24.

inspiration of God, and is profitable for doctrine, for reproof, for correction, for instruction in righteousness: That the man of God may be perfect, thoroughly furnished unto all good works" (2 Timothy 3:16). Scripture is inspired by God and is assumed in biblical and systematic theology.

1. If all Scripture is inspired by God, why is it often taken out of context?

The Biblical authors assumed the living Word of God and the role of the Holy Spirit. The Word of God should be translated through the power of the Holy Spirit, and the church should be dependent on the Holy Spirit. Doctrinal beliefs of a church should be clearly revealed and confirmed by the Holy Spirit and not emotional experience. Chester and Timmis explained,

> Spiritual experience that does not arise from God's word is not Christian experience. Other religions offer spiritual experiences. Concerts and therapy sessions can affect our emotions. Not all that passes for Christian experience is genuine. An authentic experience of the Spirit is an experience in response to the gospel.[4]

1. How do Christians confuse emotional experience with spiritual experience?

---

[4] Chester and Timmis, *Total Church, 31*

Understand the Original Meaning of the Text

It is necessary to know the historical context when articulating doctrinal beliefs. This is particularly true when preaching the Word of God. The importance of historical context is explained in *Preaching God's Word*. "Remember, the goal of our preaching is to translate the meaning of the text in the time of the biblical audience to the meaning of the text in our time, connecting this meaning in a relevant and contemporary way."[5] The truth of God and the core of doctrinal beliefs do not change, but the methods of communicating these truths may differ.

1. What are some ways to understand the historical context of the text?

Interpreting Genres

The different genres and original languages also need to be considered. Words and phrases cannot be translated word for word, and certain sayings and proverbs may have had a different meaning than they do today. Gary Bredfeldt and Lawrence Richards elaborated, "It is inspired by the Spirit of God so that it records, in its very words, God's special revelation concerning His dealings with human beings. Yet it does this using the writing skills and

---

[5] Terry Carter and G, J. Scott Duval, and J. Daniel Hays, *Preaching God's Word*, (Grand Rapids, MI: Zondervan, 2005), loc.278.

selected genres of its human authors."[6] The authors used different writing styles in different genres, such as poetry or narratives. Goldsworthy suggested that "approaching the text of the Bible in order to find out what it really says and means, needs an understanding of biblical theology."[7] Biblical theology helps decipher the original meaning of the text, knowing that each passage relates to a unified message of Jesus.

1. How do different genres affect the interpretation of passages?

Holistic Gospel

Scott McKnight argued from 1 Corinthians 15 that the gospel of Paul declared Jesus as the Messiah 'according to Scriptures.' Paul used the Scriptures from creation until Jesus returns to declare that Jesus is the promised Messiah. He went on to say that the gospels are all about Jesus, and he completes Israel's story in a way that the story is a saving story. McKnight explained that the gospel is "framed by Israel's story: the narration of the saving story of Jesus-his life, his death, his resurrection, his exaltation, and his coming again-as the completion of the Story of Israel."[8] The

---

[6] Gary J. Bredfeldt and Lawrence O. Richards, *Creative Bible Teaching*, (Chicago: Moody Publishers, 1998), loc.640.

[7] Graeme Goldsworthy, *According to Plan,* (Intervarsity Press, 2009), 19

[8] Scot McKnight, Dallas Willard, and N. T. Wright, The King Jesus Gospel: The Original Good News Revisited, (Grand Rapids, MI: Zondervan, 2016), 148.

gospel was and is to preach everything about Jesus from Genesis to Revelation and should include the summons to respond in faith, repentance, and baptism. Biblical theology ensures that doctrinal beliefs are considered within the unity of the entire gospel and that the original meaning is understood.

1. What is the gospel, according to Scott McKnight?

Understand the Application to the Reader

The meaning of the text never changes but the application may change depending on the culture and the situation of the reader. Paul wrote in his letter to the Corinthians,

> To the Jews I became like a Jew, to win the Jews. To those under the law I became like one under the law (though I myself am not under the law), so as to win those under the law. To those not having the law I became like one not having the law (though I am not free from God's law but am under Christ's law), so as to win those not having the law. To the weak I became weak, to win the weak. I have become all things to all people so that by all possible means I might save some (1Cor. 9:20-22).

As an example, certain cultures, such as in Latin American and Asian countries, are more societal and familial in contrast to individualistic cultures in Europe and North America. North Americans and Europeans are also generally more organized around time, whereas Africans and Latin Americans prioritize events. These differences may influence their understanding of

Scripture. Cultural differences are important to consider as different cultures may understand stories differently depending on their upbringing.

1. How does culture influence the interpretation of Scripture?

Narrative and Obligatory Interpretation

While all of Scripture is authoritative and the inspired Word of God, not all of Scripture should be considered directly applicable to readers today. Gordon Fee and Stuart Douglas explained, "Unless Scripture explicitly tells us that we must do something, what is only narrated or described does not function in a normative (i.e. obligatory) way-unless it can be demonstrated on other grounds that the author intended it to function in this way."[9]

As an example, the Book of Acts records how and where the early church met. These are useful observations for the church, but this is not a required model of the church. Jesus does, however, explicitly command his followers to baptize believers and observe the Lord's supper in remembrance of death as a payment for one's sins. These are explicit commands for the church.

1. What is another example of a biblical passage that is narrative and not an explicate command?

---

[9] Gordon, D Fee and Douglas Stuart. How to Read the Bible for All Its Worth. (Grand Rapids: Zondervan, 2003), 119.

1.3
CASE STUDY: BIBLICAL THEOLOGY

Some biblical teachings and doctrines have been controversial as they are interpreted differently. Considering that biblical theology interprets Scripture as a whole and not in isolation, how would you build a case for one of the following controversial topics?

1. Women teaching in the church
2. Washing feet
3. Drinking alcohol
4. Women wearing pants
5. Eternal salvation

2.1

HEART OF THE DISCIPLE: FEAR

Fear is a weapon of the enemy to prevent the expansion of God's kingdom. Fear of failure and uncertainty prevent ministry leaders and believers from taking risks and trusting God to provide through all circumstances. Since Adam and Eve hid from God in fear, Satan has been using fear to disrupt our relationship with God.

Fear is an unbelief that God is in control over every circumstance. While Jesus promises tribulation, he is able to do abundantly more than we could ask for (Eph. 3:20).

I. Not all fear is from the enemy.

Proverbs 9:10, **Ps. 111:10 (The fear of the Lord is the beginning of wisdom)**

Meditate on Ps. 111:10

1.How is the fear of the Lord different from fear of the enemy?

II. Believers have overcome fear.

2 Tim. 1:7 (God gave us a spirit of power, love and self-control), 1 John 5:5, **John 16:33 (we have peace in tribulation as Jesus has overcome the world),** James 2:20-21 (Christ suffered for you as an example)

17

Meditate on John 16:33

1. Jesus promised that there would be tribulation but that he has overcome the world. How does this affect your approach to uncertainty?

III. Believers have access to the power of the Holy Spirit.
John 14:15-17 (Jesus promised the Holy Spirit), **1 John 4:13 (Jesus has given us his Spirit)**
Meditate on 1 John 4:13

1. How does the Spirit empower believers to overcome fear?

IV. The light shines in the darkness.
1 John 1:5-10 (Walk in the light. If we say we have no sin, we deceive ourselves), Eph. 5:12-14 (light exposes things done in secret)
Meditate on 1 John 1:5-10

1. The light exposes things done in secret. What do you need to confess to God or a trusted friend to expose the fear in your life?

2. What are some things that you can start doing today to walk closer with Jesus in the light?

V. Faith overcomes doubt and fear.
Heb. 11:1-3 (Faith is the assurance of things hoped for but unseen), Matt. 17:14-21 (Faith as small as a mustard seed will move mountains), **Eph. 3:14-21 (God is able to do abundantly more than we ask according to the power within us)**, Mark 9:24 (Lord, help my unbelief), 1 John 4:18 (love casts out fear)

Meditate on Eph. 3:14-21

1. How will you pray differently knowing that God is able to do abundantly more than you can ask for?

2.2

CULTURAL DIFFERENCES

Not right, Not wrong, Just different
Wallace Mitchell III

Visiting other cultures is a beautiful experience. Learning new languages, customs and tasting new foods enriches one's life experience. Visiting other cultures can also create misunderstanding and confusion if one has preconceived beliefs about new cultures. David Livermore illustrated in the picture below that most of the experiences one has with new cultures are superficial. Understanding cultures requires time and effort to learn the deeper values and the unconscious stereotypes and ethnocentrism that one may have.

Three Categories of Human Behavior[10]

UNIVERSAL

CULTURAL

Cultural Artifacts and Systems
Art, clothing, food, money, customs, gestures, etc.

Cultural Values and Assumptions
Unconscious, taken-for-granted beliefs, perceptions, and feelings

PERSONAL

1. What are some ways to learn the deeper values of new cultures?

Communication Styles

Intentions to communicate the gospel in love could be interpreted as offensive without cross-cultural consideration. Livermore explained, "The desire to treat other people with honor and respect doesn't automatically mean our behavior comes across as dignifying and kind."[11] Cultures that normally communicate

---

[10] David Livermore, *Leading with Cultural Intelligence: The New Secret to Success*, (New York, NY: American Management Association, 2015), 74.

[11] Ibid., 18

directly, may intend to be respectful and kind but are received as disrespectful by cultures that communicate indirectly. Duane Elmer discussed the concept of direct and indirect communication, which he calls straight or curved.[12] Western cultures use linear, direct logic when communicating. Direct communication normally goes straight to the point without flattery. The objective is to communicate the point to be made. Eastern cultures normally use spiraled, indirect language. The objective is to build trust in the relationship and prevent shaming a person. A lack of understanding of these styles of communication leads to misunderstanding the motivation of the communicator. Direct communicators may perceive indirect communication as deceptive and indirect communicators may interpret direct communicators as rude and inconsiderate.

1. How would you describe the communication style of your culture?

2. How would you describe the communication style of the culture you intend to serve in?

3. How would these communication styles cause conflict?

---

[12] Duane H. Elmer, Cross-Cultural Connections: Stepping Out and Fitting in Around the World, (Downers Grove, IL: Intervarsity Press, 2002), 142.

Facial Expressions

Facial expressions are an important consideration when communicating the gospel in global cultures. If one is impatient or frustrated, facial expressions communicate a lack of value and respect for the other person. Individualist cultures may not be offended by facial expressions as people are encouraged to express one's feelings. Collectivist cultures encourage people to honor others and to hide their feelings so as not to cause shame. One's interpretations of facial expressions may not be correct as the other person may be hiding their feelings. This is helpful information when communicating the gospel to others. Signs of disinterest may be discouraging when they are listening but not showing any interest. On the contrary, signs of interest may incorrectly be interpreted as the other person understanding when they do not. Garrick Bailey and James Peoples explain that "speech is affected by how situations are culturally defined and the particular individuals who are present."[13] When communicating cross-culturally, one needs to carefully assess the other person and how they may be interpreting what is communicated.

Personal distance should be considered. Some cultures prefer to be close to one another when speaking with a hand on the shoulder or holding hands. While this may be regarded as a

---

[13] Garrick Bailey and James Peoples, *Essentials of Cultural Anthropology*, (Belmont, CA: Wadsworth/Cengage Learning, 2014), 51.

romantic gesture in Western cultures, in some cultures, it is a sign of trust. Western cultures generally prefer to communicate about an arm's length apart from one another. In Middle Eastern and Eastern cultures, interactions between males and females may be inappropriate. Do your research and follow the lead of your hosts.

1. How much do you read into body language and facial expressions?
2. How aware are you of the body language you communicate to others?

Ethnocentrism

Ethnocentrism is a challenge for the church in communicating the gospel cross-culturally. Ethnocentrism is the conscious or unconscious view that one's culture is better than others. Most people have a degree of ethnocentrism, as it is normal to be proud of one's ethnicity. Ethnocentrism is harmful to the church when it causes division and offends others. In most cases, ethnocentrism results in miscommunication and minor disputes, which may be resolved. In extreme cases, ethnocentrism is oppressive and damaging to the church and the gospel. Paul Hiebert noted, "Racism is an extreme form of ethnocentrism that is particularly oppressive."[14] The church needs to strive for unity cross-culturally. Paul wrote, "There is neither Jew nor Greek, there is neither slave nor free, there is no male and female, for you are all one in Christ Jesus" (Gal. 3:28). Multi-ethnic churches and diversity need to be encouraged, but the churches common identity is in Christ.

Improving one's cultural intelligence makes one more effective in adapting to other ethnicities and integrating one's worldview with others. Stella Ting-Toomey and Leeva Chung explained,

> As human beings, we display ethnocentric tendencies for three reasons: (1) we tend to define what goes on in our own culture as natural and correct and what goes on in other cultures as unnatural and incorrect; (2) we tend to perceive ingroup values, customs, norms, and roles as universally applicable; and (3) we tend to experience distance from the outgroup, especially when our group identity is threatened or under attack.[15]

Being motivated to learn and interact with other cultures and improving one's knowledge and understanding of other cultures are needed for the church to communicate the gospel cross-culturally.

1. What is one thing you like and one you dislike about your culture compared to others?

---

[14] Paul G. Hiebert, The Gospel in Human Contexts: Anthropological Explorations for Contemporary Missions, (Grand Rapids, MI: Baker Academic, 2009), 63.

[15] Stella Ting-Toomey and Leeva C. Chung, *Understanding Intercultural Communication*, (Oxford, NY: Oxford University Press, 2012), 163.

2. What is one thing you like and one thing you dislike about the culture you intend to serve in?

3. How intentional are you to interact with other cultures?

Stereotypes

Stereotypes are expectations that one has of other cultures. There is often some truth in stereotypes as cultures form certain behaviors and identities. Stereotypes may be helpful for churches as they develop strategies and communication styles for communicating the gospel cross-culturally. While adapting one's communication and using this knowledge to interpret communication in cross-cultural settings is useful, one should be aware that all individuals communicate differently, and generalizations can be misleading. Short and infrequent interactions with cultures may reinforce stereotypes that are incorrect. Churches that send short-term mission trips need to be aware of forming incorrect stereotypes. Howell and Williams noted the dangers of cross-cultural short-term trips.

> The trip may provide a false sense of understanding and connection when a great deal more time and engagement is necessary for real knowledge. A short trip is often just long enough to have stereotypes reinforced, prejudices confirmed, or judgments strengthened. Truly connecting with people in other cultures in the course of a two-week trip requires an understanding of the context and an ability

to engage people in ways that fit with the culture of the hosts rather than the preferences of the guests.[16]

Frequent interactions with other cultures are needed to form true opinions of individuals and other cultures.

Churches communicating the gospel cross-culturally need to understand that they are primarily relating to individuals as parts of a culture. Love and respect are the foundations of relationships. Jesus will be known by the way the church loves one another regardless of diversity. "By this everyone will know that you are my disciples if you love one another" (John 13:35).

1. What stereotypes do people have of your culture?

2. What stereotypes do people have of the culture you intend to serve in?

Cultural Values

Cross-cultural discipleship requires learning the worldviews and values of the new culture and knowing the values of one's own culture. While culture shock is unavoidable, cross-cultural preparation will enable deeper communication and relationships.

Cultural values defined (adapted from Livermore and Elmer)

---

[16] Brian M. Howell and Jenell Williams Paris, Introducing Cultural Anthropology: A Christian Perspective, (Grand Rapids, MI: Baker Academic, 2011), 258.

Short Term	Long Term
Emphasis on immediate outcomes.	**Emphasis on long-term outcomes.**

Short term _____ long term

Formal Education	Informal Education
The use of schools, book, and professionally trained teachers to educate youth.	The emphasis on wisdom passed to youth from extended family members, parents and siblings.

Formal _____ Informal

Formal Legal System	Informal Legal System
A very formalized system, which is chronicled in things like a written constitution and laws.	Although less formalized, simple legal systems are still binding and are passed along though conventional wisdom. Citizens and visitors are presumed to understand and follow the rules.

Formal _____ Informal

Rational Religious System	Mystical Religious System
The emphasis is on finding reason-based scientific answers to the supernatural with a focus on individual responsibility and work ethic.	The emphasis is on supernatural powers, both good and evil, that control day-to-day events and life.

Rational _____ Mystical

Solid Artistic Systems	Fluid Artistic Systems
A preference for clean, tight boundaries that emphasize precision and straight lines.	A preference for more fluid, indiscriminate lines with an emphasis on ebb and flow and flexibility.

Solid _____ Fluid

Event Time Orientation	Clock Time Orientation
Emphasizes social relationship and values spontaneity.	Emphasizes punctuality, being industrious and values efficiency.
Examples:	**Examples:**
Brazil	Australia
India	China
United Arab Emirates	United States

Event _____ Time

Low Context	High Context
Emphasizes explicit words and values direct communication.	Emphasizes roles and implicit understanding and values indirect communication.
Examples:	**Examples:**
United States	Brazil
Israel	China
Australia	United Arab Emirates

Low Context _____ High Context

Individualism	Collectivism
Emphasizes "I" and individual identity.	Emphasizes "we" and group identity (e.g., family, work group organization, tribe).
Prefers individual decisions and working alone.	Prefers group decisions and working with others.
Examples:	**Examples:**
United States	China
Australia	Columbia
United Kingdom	United Arab Emirates

Individualism _____ Collectivism

Low Power Distance	High Power Distance
Expects that all should have equal rights.	Expects power holders to be entitled to privileges.
Is willing to question and challenge the views of superiors.	Is willing to support and accept the views of superiors.
Examples:	**Examples:**
Israel	China
Austria	United Arab Emirates
United Kingdom	France (United States is in the middle)

Low Power _____ High Power

Low Uncertainty Avoidance	High Uncertainty Avoidance
Prefers few rules, little structure and few guidelines.	Prefers written rules, structure, and guidelines.
Tolerates unstructured and unpredictable situations.	Is uncomfortable with unstructured or unpredictable situations.
Examples:	**Examples:**
Jamaica	Greece
Sweden	United Arab Emirates
Malaysia	Japan
(China and USA are near the middle)	

Low Uncertainty _____ High Uncertainty

2.3

CULTURAL VALUES DEFINED

1. Plot yourself on each of the above continuums.

2. From what you know about your target culture, how are you different?

3. How could these differences cause conflict?

3.1

HEART OF THE DISCIPLE: HUMILITY

Jesus desires humility and sacrifice to follow him. "If anyone would come after me, let him deny himself and take up his cross daily and follow me. For whoever will save his life will lose it, but whoever loses his life for my sake will save it" (Luke 9:23-24). Cross-cultural discipleship requires humility in demonstrating Christ's humility, and God uses people most when they humble themselves before God and others.

I. Jesus demonstrated humility

Phil. 2:1-11 (Jesus took the nature of a servant in being made in human likeness)

Meditate on Phil. 2:1-11

1. How can followers of Jesus demonstrate the same kind of humility as Jesus did?

II. Humility is necessary to receive and enjoy abundant life.

John 13:1-20 (You are blessed if you wash the feet of others),

Matt. 23:12 (Whoever humbles himself will be exalted)

Meditate on Matt. 23:12

1.How is it possible to be exalted in humility?

III. Love is demonstrated through humility.

John 13:34-35, 15:12-13 (Jesus commanded his disciples to love one another as he loved us), Col. 3:12-14 (Paul told the church to put on love and humility among other characteristics)

Meditate on John 13:34-35

1. How can the church love one another as Jesus loved you?

2. Why will people be attracted to the church by the way they love another?

IV. Humility is needed for total dependence on God.

1 Peter 5:6-11 (Humble yourselves and cast all your anxieties on him), Proverbs 3:34 (God gives favor to the humble), James 4:6-8 (God gives grace to the humble)

Meditate on 1 Peter 5:6-11

1. Peter tells the church to humble themselves before God, casting their anxieties on him. Why does casting your anxieties on God require humility?

2. Why does God allow his people to suffer before restoring them?

V. Humility is dying to your personal desires and living for Jesus.

2 Cor. 5:14-15 (Believers no longer live for themselves but for Jesus), **Luke 9:57-62 (Following Jesus is leaving the comforts of home)**, Luke 9:23-27 (Jesus told his followers to pick up their crosses and follow him), Luke 12:34 (For where your treasure is, there your heart will be also)

Meditate on Luke 9:57-62

1.What comforts are preventing you from following Jesus wholeheartedly?

3.2

CONTEXTUALIZATION

As followers of Jesus take the gospel to the nations, they need to understand other cultures in order to communicate the gospel effectively. Global cultures may share common aspects such as economy, business practices, and English as a globally recognized language. Local communities, however, retain their traditions and worldviews as they have values and beliefs that are core to their identities. The globalization of cultures is the tip of the iceberg and does not reflect a culture's true identity. To effectively operate and communicate cross-culturally, one needs to understand the local culture as well as the global impact on culture. Livermore explained, "Today's organization and its leaders must be both local and global, or "glocal," in understanding and serving customers."[17] One does not need to completely integrate into a culture to effectively communicate the gospel, but the gospel presentation may need to be adapted for the gospel to be understood.

1. What are the advantages of globalization?

2. What are the disadvantages of globalization?

---

[17] Livermore, *Leading with Cultural Intelligence*, 15.

3. How does globalization influence cross-cultural discipleship?

Transcultural Mediation

Globalization of cultures is changing the methods of gospel communication. In the past, missionaries like Hudson Taylor and William Carey left their homes and possessions permanently. Missionaries dedicated their lives to new cultures and became enculturated into the new culture. The time and expense of travel made it challenging to return to their home countries. The convenience of air travel and communication via the Internet allows modern missionaries to remain connected to their home cultures, which disrupts their language learning and integration into a new culture. Some may consider this a negative consequence of modern missions, but Paul Hiebert believes transcultural mediation is beneficial. Hiebert explains the missionary culture of the future as missionaries are able to move between cultures with greater ease than in the past. "They must be truly bicultural or transcultural people, living in different worlds but not fully at home in any of them."[18] This is a relevant view for present cross-cultural workers.

---

[18] Paul G. Hiebert, *The Gospel in Human Contexts: Anthropological Explorations for Contemporary Missions*, (Grand Rapids, MI: Baker Academic, 2009), 120.

1. What are the advantages of being conveniently connected to one's home country?

2. What are the consequences of not integrating into the new culture?

Becoming All Things to All People

Complete integration is not possible. One will gain parts of another culture and lose parts of their home culture, but regardless of how long one lives in another culture, they will never be completely integrated. Paul understood this well as he adapted to the cultures to whom he was communicating (1 Cor. 9:20-22).

Paul did not attempt to become the people to whom he was communicating but became like them and adapted the presentation accordingly. Acts 17 records how Paul adapted his message to the Greeks on Mars Hill. The presentation is adapted to the beliefs and values of the audience. Scott Duval and Daniel Hays expanded on this in their description of the Book of Acts.

> When preaching to Jews, the preachers usually use Scripture and the history of Israel as the basis of the appeal (chs. 2, 3, 13). When preaching to Gentiles the preachers build a bridge by appealing to God as creator (chs. 14, 17). On the topic of evangelistic preaching we can say that Acts teaches us to hold fast to the core message of the gospel, but we must be willing to tailor our presentation depending on the nature of our audience.[19]

---

[19] Scott J. Duval and J. Daniel Hays, *Grasping God's Word*, (Grand Rapids: Zondervan, 2012), .305.

1. How can one adapt the gospel to a different culture without changing the meaning of the message?

Multi-Ethnic Churches

Biblical transcultural mediation is valuable as one shares cultural values and worldviews from their home culture while also learning and gaining cultural values and worldviews from the new cultures. Together, these cultures form a global culture based on a Biblical worldview as the foundation. Multi-ethnic churches and international churches attempt to integrate different values and worldviews. Cultural differences are, however, important to consider as diverse cultures may understand Bible stories differently depending on their upbringing and traditions.

1. What are the challenges of multi-ethnic churches?

2. How can these challenges be overcome?

Muslim Contextualization

John Travis developed the C spectrum, which ranges from C1, in which the Muslim Background Believer (MBB) adapts to a traditional church using a language different from the surrounding Muslim community and reflects a different culture which in most cases is Western. The culture is vastly different from the Muslim culture, and the MBB is undoubtedly identified as Christian by the

Muslim community. The C spectrum gradually becomes more contextualized until C6, which is secret or underground followers of Jesus with little or no visible community.

(John Travis, EMQ 34:3 (Oct, 1998)

C-1: Traditional church using language and cultural forms which are foreign to the local Muslim population.	*Think of themselves as*
C-2: Traditional church using cultural forms which are foreign to the local Muslim population but using the common, daily language.	*Christians*
C-3: Contextualized Christ-centered communities using local language and non-religious cultural forms.	*Muslims understand them to be Christians*
C-4: Contextualized Christ-centered communities using biblically permissible cultural and Islamic forms. *Self-identified as "Followers of Jesus." Muslims perceive them to be "a kind of Christian"*	

C-5: Christ-centered communities of

"Messianic Muslims" who have accepted

Jesus as Lord and Savior using biblically

acceptable and reinterpreted Islamic

forms.

Self-identified as "Muslim Followers of

Jesus."

Muslims perceive them to be "a strange

kind of Muslim."

C-6: Small Christ-centered communities of

secret/underground believers.

Private followers of Jesus. Perceived to

be Muslims.

C5 and C6 believers worship Jesus in secret under fear of persecution, identify themselves as Muslims, and are perceived as Muslims by the Muslim community. They worship in Mosques and may acknowledge the authority of the Qur'an and other Holy books along with the Bible. It is debated to what extent an MBB can continue to live in an Islamic culture and still be a follower of Jesus. Phil Parshall believes that C5 practices are unethical forms of Christianity, particularly as praying in a Mosque is a sacred Islamic ritual, even if the MBB is secretly praying to Jesus.[20]

John J. Travis disagrees and believes that C5 MBBs are "saved by faith in Christ, not by religious affiliation."[21] He explained that C5 MBBs understand the identity and work of Christ, and over half understand the Trinity. Regarding the Qur'an, Travis agrees with Parshall that followers of Jesus cannot affirm all that is written in it.

In the same way that many Christians are only Christian by name and not theology, Islam is often a cultural identity. Many Muslims identify as Muslim but do not practice or believe in the teaching of Islam and the Qur'an. Travis explained that "the gap between personal commitment and official theology is one of the things that allows for some Muslims to remain a part of their community and still follow Jesus as Lord and Savior."[22] They can culturally identify as Muslims while being true followers of Jesus.

1. Considering that MBBs live under fear of persecution, how integrated can they remain in Muslim cultures while still being considered followers of Jesus?

---

[20] Phil Parshall, "Going Too Far?"," *Perspectives on the World Christian Movement.* 4th ed. Pasadena, (CA: William Carey, 2009), 666. .

[21] John J. Travis, "Must all Muslims Leave 'Islam' to Follow Jesus?" *Perspectives on the World Christian Movement.* 4th ed. Pasadena, (CA: William Carey, 2009), 668.

[22] John J. Travis, "Appropriate Approaches in Muslim Contexts." *Appropriate Christianity,* (CA: William Carey, 2005) 405.

Contextualizing the Gospel

There is no decontextualized gospel. The moment one translates the Bible, contextualization begins. Forms of communication may be understood in some cultures but not in others. Forms of communication include language, illustrations, humor, and clothing. Using humor may be engaging in some cultures but offensive in others. Tim Keller observed, "Every form of gospel presentation will either over-adapt or under-adapt to a culture."[23] Over-adapting to culture may result in diluting the message when the communicator does not ask the listener to repent of sinful behaviors or what to do according to the gospel. Over-adapting results in syncretism. This is common in churches that emphasize the grace of God and minimize his just character. Under-adapting to a culture results in legalism as the communicator is not flexible and imposes cultural norms and not gospel norms on another culture. Legalism was what Jesus rebuked the Pharisees for, as they imposed laws on people without understanding the purpose of the laws. Some churches are more concerned with following laws and lose focus on developing a

---

[23] Sam Chan, 2018, "GETTING OUR ACCENT RIGHT: Recognizing and Making the Most of an Enculturated Gospel," Christianity Today 62 (5): 50–56. https://search-ebscohost-com.ezproxy.liberty.edu/login.aspx?direct=true&db=lsdar&AN=ATLAiE58180528001124&site=ehost-live&scope=site.

loving relationship with God. The ideal objective is to balance under-adapting and over-adapting with contextualization.

1. How do you balance under-contextualizing and over-contextualizing the gospel?

Interpreting Stories

Cultural differences are important to consider, as different cultures may understand stories differently depending on their upbringing. This is especially important in the parables that Jesus told. As an example, in the story of *The Prodigal Son*, Eastern familial cultures may focus on the shame that the son brought to his family when he asked for his inheritance and then squandered it irresponsibly. They may identify more with the proud son who was loyal to his father. Western individualistic cultures may identify more with the irresponsible son who was welcomed back by his father. The culture should determine how one teaches this parable. Jesus taught these parables to Middle Eastern cultures that are very different from modern Western cultures.

1. How would you teach Bible stories to an oral, indirect culture?

3.3
CASE STUDY: TO CATCH A THIEF

Mike and Sandy were missionaries in a South American country, where Mike served as a medical doctor in a mission clinic. One morning when Mike was away, and the local nurses came to open the clinic, they discovered there had been a break-in. Muddy footprints led to an open bathroom window. The clinic cash box was gone. When Mike returned, the nurses told him that they had reported the theft to the two village government authorities, men who served as the local equivalents to a sheriff and a judge. The two men also happened to be members of the local evangelical church. Mike knew they wouldn't have sophisticated scientific equipment to do a criminal investigation but trusted that they would have culturally appropriate ways to follow up on the crime and discover the thief.

Several days later, Mike was talking with one of the nurses and noticed a dirty brick with a plastic bag behind it in the corner of the room where the cash box had been.

"What's that?" he asked the nurse.

"Oh, that's the sheriff's plan for discovering the thief," she answered.

To Mike's shock, when he pulled away the plastic bag, he discovered a human skull with a crown of thorns around the cranium, two cigarettes stuck between the teeth, coca leaves sprinkled around the base, and wax stains on the brick where candles had been burned. The two officials had gone to the local cemetery and dug up some bones. Then they had arranged the skull and other paraphernalia to perform a ritual that they believed would make the thief sick and so force him to return the money. The story is true, but the names have been changed.[24]

1. What may have led these Christian believers to perform this animistic practice?

2. How would you advise Mike and Sandy to respond?

3. How might appropriate biblical contextualization address this issue?

---

[24] Craig Ott and Stephen Strauss, *Encountering Theology of Mission.* (Grand Rapids, MI: Baker, 2010) 291.

4.1
HEART OF THE DISCIPLE: FORGIVENESS

Living in this fallen world, no person is immune to hurt and suffering. You have been hurt directly or indirectly by others and may have caused suffering to others close to you. You may not be in a place where you are ready to forgive, but as you walk with Jesus and receive his forgiveness for you, the Holy Spirit will prepare your heart to forgive.

Living and working cross-culturally brings blessings and joy, but there will also be suffering from unmet expectations and deliberate harm against you. When past hurt and suffering has not been resolved, the resentment carries with you into a new culture, and those resentments continue to build as one encounters disappointment and harm. Jesus came that you may have abundant life and not have to live with resentment and anger from an unforgiving heart.

I. Forgiveness is part of a believer's identity in Christ.
Col. 3:12-17, Eph. 4:32 (Forgive as the Lord has forgiven you), Heb. 8:12 (He will remember our sins no more), **Ps. 103:1-12 (God is loving, merciful, compassionate and forgiving)**
Meditate on Ps. 103:1-12

1. What was your view of God growing up?

2. How does this differ from the view that God is a loving, compassionate, and merciful Father?

3. What past experiences do you need to invite Jesus into to receive his forgiveness?

II. You are forgiven when you forgive others.

Matt. 6:14-15 (Forgive and you will be forgiven), Luke 6:27-36 (Love your enemies and expect nothing in return), Rom. 12:14-21 (Overcome evil with good), **1 John 4:20 (whoever loves God must also love his brother)**

Meditate on 1 John 4:20

1. How is loving and forgiving others related to loving God and receiving forgiveness?

III. Jesus came to heal the brokenhearted and set the captives free.

Luke 4:17-19 (Jesus proclaimed liberty to the captives), Is. 61 (Jesus came to bind up the brokenhearted), Phil. 2:13 (God works in you for his good pleasure), Ps. 103:3-4 (God forgives and heals), **1 Peter 2:24-25 (By his wounds you have been healed)**, 1 Peter 5:6-11 (Cast all your anxieties on him)

Meditate on 1 Peter 2:24-25

1. Is there any hurt, unforgiveness, anxiety, or resentment that Jesus is inviting you to release?

IV. Guard your heart continually.

Proverbs 4:23, 24:3 (Keep your heart with vigilance), Eph. 4:11-16 (spiritual maturation is a lifelong process), Jer. 17:9-10 (The heart is deceitful), Rom. 13:14 (Put on Jesus and make no provision for the flesh)

Meditate on Proverbs 4:23

1. How can you guard your heart against deceitfulness?

Healing of the Heart

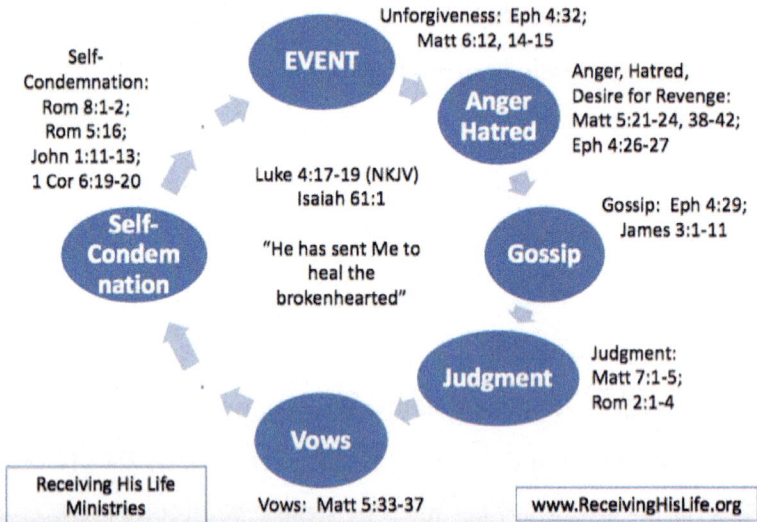

Self-Condemnation: Rom 8:1-2; Rom 5:16; John 1:11-13; 1 Cor 6:19-20

EVENT

Unforgiveness: Eph 4:32; Matt 6:12, 14-15

Anger Hatred

Anger, Hatred, Desire for Revenge: Matt 5:21-24, 38-42; Eph 4:26-27

Self-Condemnation

Luke 4:17-19 (NKJV) Isaiah 61:1

"He has sent Me to heal the brokenhearted"

Gossip

Gossip: Eph 4:29; James 3:1-11

Judgment

Judgment: Matt 7:1-5; Rom 2:1-4

Vows

Receiving His Life Ministries

Vows: Matt 5:33-37

www.ReceivingHisLife.org

V. An unforgiving heart is a vicious cycle.

1. Who do you need to forgive to break the cycle?

4.2

CULTURE SHOCK

Culture shock is the frustration one experiences from entering a new culture and not experiencing what was expected. Kalervo Oberg, who has studied culture shock extensively, says that culture shock is the "anxiety that results from losing all the familiar signs and symbols that help us understand a situation."[25] Cross-cultural interpersonal relationships may be disappointing as one is not familiar with the unspoken rules of the culture, and one is considered an outsider for not being familiar with the rules, language, and history. While culture shock occurs on short-term trips, it is more apparent in long-term assignments. It is not only associated with international travel, but also domestically, where cultures are different from one's home culture.

1. How have you experienced culture shock domestically or internationally?

---

[25] Kalvero Oberg, "Culture Shock: Adjustment to New Cultural Environments," Practical Anthropology 7, no. 4 (1967): 177.

Culture Adjustment Cycle

Culture shock is complicated and will affect people on the same team or in the same family differently. The cycle is normally a twelve-month process but could be longer. The process begins with the honeymoon stage. The new culture is exciting as one explores new relationships, food, and places. The process then moves to rejection. At this stage, one withdraws socially and prefers to socialize with people from their home culture. One experiences anger toward people of a foreign culture as it is interpreted as different and bad. Gossip occurs among people of similar cultures, mocking the foreign culture as different and foolish. The next stage is the recovery stage, as one begins to tolerate the new culture. One understands that culture is different but reasonable and opens up to personal interaction. The process is repeated when re-entering one's home culture and is known as reverse culture shock.

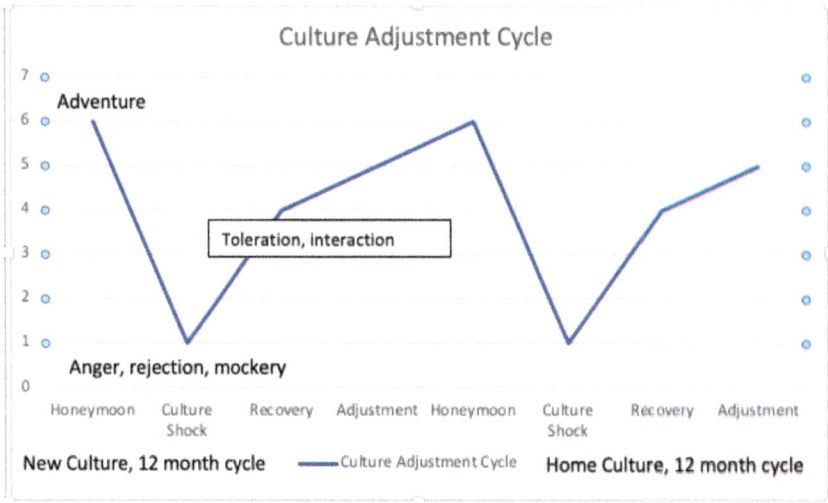

Culture Adjustment Cycle

Adventure

Toleration, interaction

Anger, rejection, mockery

Honeymoon · Culture Shock · Recovery · Adjustment · Honeymoon · Culture Shock · Recovery · Adjustment

New Culture, 12 month cycle ——Culture Adjustment Cycle **Home Culture, 12 month cycle**

1. How can you prepare psychologically for inevitable culture shock?

Expectations

Unmet expectations are one reason which leads to culture shock. Duane Elmer notes, "The great common door through which most forms of negativity enter is pre-mature expectations." Expectations could be on a conscious or sub-conscious level, and unmet expectations can lead to resentment and judgment. Elmer advises to stop, analyze the situation, suspend judgment, and consider why the situation occurred.

1. What expectations do you have of your target culture?

2. What expectations do your target culture expect of you?

3. How can you communicate these expectations clearly?

Spiritual Warfare

The enemy attacks believers in isolation as they are vulnerable. Community is an essential part of spiritual growth as well as a defense against the enemy. Cross-cultural workers are particularly exposed as they are normally away from spiritual community and confront unfamiliar stresses of adapting to new cultures and languages (1 Chron. 21, **1 Peter 5:6-11**). Satan attacks your identity as he wants you to believe you are not equipped to be a spiritual leader, you are not good enough, he is punishing you, or you missed God's call. Elmer wrote that Satan will lie to:

1. Discourage you from getting involved in ministry

2. Rob you of the excitement of being in a new culture

3. Disrupt your learning of the new culture

4. Blame others

5. Focus on yourself and not the people you want to serve

Remind yourself of your identity in Christ, reject fear by walking closely with Jesus through the power of the Holy Spirit, allow God to work through your humility and weaknesses, and forgive those who hurt and offend you.

1. Laugh at yourself

2. Others do not expect you to know everything

3. Take breaks and explore neighboring countries and towns

4. Give grace to those who are experiencing the culture differently

5. Stay committed to joy and thankfulness

6. Set reasonable expectations

7. Do not come home too soon! You will get through this

Approach	The Facts of Life Abroad (inevitables)	Coping Strategies (responses)	Results
Openness Acceptance Trust	CULTURAL DIFFERENCES — FRUSTRATION CONFUSION	CHOICES — Observe Listen Inquire	Rapport & Understanding
Fear Suspicion Inflexibility	TENSION EMBARRASSMENT	Criticize Rationalize Withdraw	Alienation & Isolation

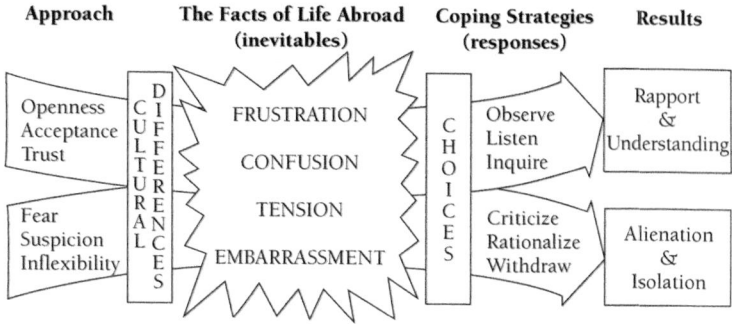

(Elmer, Cross-cultural Connections)

Meditate on 1 Peter 5:6-11.

1. How will you increase your awareness of spiritual attacks?

2. How are you intentionally surrounding yourself with the Christian community?

Missionary Care

Sending churches and mission agencies need to be caring for the physical and spiritual well-being of missionaries so that they have the capacity to care for others physically and spiritually. David Joannes noted that 71 percent of missionaries leave the field or preventable reasons and lack of missionary care is high on the st.[26] Missionaries often feel isolated and abandoned.

William Carey went to India and was considered as the father of modern missions. He attempted great things for God but understood that he could not do it alone. "After hearing an account of the spiritual needs of India, the secretary of the meeting remarked: 'There is a gold mine in India, but it seems almost as deep as the center of the earth. Who will venture to explore it?' 'I will venture to go down,' said Carey, 'but remember that you must hold the ropes.'"[27] Carey appreciated the value of support from sending churches and mission agencies in global engagement. He convinced the missionary society to send reinforcements and "in 1799 Joshua and Hannah Marshman and William Ward arrived to help him."[28] Together they cared for the spiritual and humanitarian needs of the Indians as they planted churches, trained Indian pastors, and started schools. Contemporary missions can learn and apply these principles from the father of modern missions.

Apart from sending churches and agencies, cross-cultural workers need a strong care team. This team will operate as financial advisors, offer emotional and spiritual support, pray

David Joannes, *The Mind of the Missionary: What Global Kingdom Workers Tell Us About Thriving on Mission*, (Within Reach Global Inc., 2018), 131

John M. Terry and Robert L. Gallagher, Encountering the History of Missions: from the Early Church to Today, (Grand Rapids, MI: Baker, 2017), 247.

Terry et. al., Encountering the History of Missions, 247.

consistently, maintain contact with the missionary and their partners, and offer logistical support upon re-entry or home assignments. The Great Commandment is applicable to those who stay as well as those who are sent.

> For everyone who calls on the name of the Lord will be saved. How then will they call on him whom they have not believed? And how are they to believe in him of whom they have never heard? And how are they to hear without someone preaching? And how are they to preach unless they are sent? As it is written, "How beautiful are the feet of those who preach the good news!" (Rom. 10:13-15)

Cross-cultural workers need a strong support team that will help them combat spiritual warfare and culture shock.

1. If you are the sender, how can you support the missionaries in your church?

2. If you are being sent, who are you including in your care team?

4.3
CASE STUDY: CULTURE SHOCK

While living in another country, an American took his car to the local mechanic. Even though the mechanic spoke basic English, the American wanted to impress him with his language ability, so he used the local dialect to say, "My engine is not working well; please change the spark plugs." The mechanic, on hearing this in his own language, doubled over in laughter, as did some others who overheard. The American was quite embarrassed but resisted the temptation to take his car and leave. Instead, he said, "What did I say that you found so funny?" The mechanic, still trying to control himself, managed to say, "You told me that your car will not give birth and I must change its bananas," and he began to laugh again, as did the others.

Each time the American saw the mechanic, the mechanic broke into laughter. Later, someone asked the American, "Don't you feel embarrassed that this person always laughs at you when you meet?" The American had a wise answer, "I do a little, but I prefer to look at it this way. Every time we meet, I bring a little cheer into his life, and I think that is a good thing."[29]

1. How would you respond in this situation?

---

[29] Elmer, *Cross-Cultural Connections*, 49.

5.1
HEART OF DISCIPLE: DEPENDENCE ON THE HOLY SPIRIT

The danger in missions is for missionaries to become dependent on programs and humanitarian work and neglect their dependence on the Holy Spirit. Before Jesus ascended to heaven, he promised the presence of the Holy Spirit to his disciples.

> He said to them: "It is not for you to know the dates or times the Father has set by his own authority. But you will receive power when the Holy Spirit comes on you, and you will be my witnesses in Jerusalem, and in all Judea and Samaria and to the ends of the earth" (Acts: 1:7-8).

The purpose of God's people is to know God more deeply and to make him known among all the nations. Commenting on Acts 1:7-8, Darrell Bock wrote that "it is for mission that the Spirit is sent."[30] It is only through the power of the Holy Spirit that believers can be witnesses of Jesus, and every believer is required to be a witness in order to make him known to the ends of the

---

[30] Darrell Bock, Baker Exegetical Commentary on the New Testament: Acts, (Grand Rapids: MI: Baker Academic, 2007), 70.

earth. Every believer can be a witness to where God has placed them.

It would be foolish and arrogant to believe that the church and the missionaries it sends can build a church and mission model based on its own knowledge and abilities. David Platt expanded on the role of the Holy Spirit.

> The church I lead could have the least gifted people, the least talented people, the fewest leaders, and the least money, and this church under the power of the Holy Spirit could still shake the nations for his glory. The reality is that the church I lead can accomplish more during the next month in the power of God's spirit than we can in the next hundred years apart from his provision. His power is so superior to ours. Why do we not desperately seek it?[31]

The Holy Spirit not only gives the church knowledge and abilities to carry out the work God has planned, but it is only through the work of the Holy Spirit that people will respond to the gospel and put their trust and faith in Jesus as their Lord and Savior. Reliance on the Holy Spirit in any type of ministry, especially missions, is a clear teaching of Jesus, and every believer has the power of the Holy Spirit.

I. God's power is demonstrated through your weakness.
2 Cor. 12:9-10 (God's power is made perfect in weakness), John 16:33 (There is tribulation, but Jesus has overcome the world), Rom. 6:11 (You are dead to sin and alive in Christ), 1 Cor. 1:27-31

---

[31] David Platt, *Radical,* (Colorado Springs: Multnomah Books, 2010), 54.

God chose what is weak to shame the strong), 2 Cor. 12. 1-2 (Paul
was given a thorn to prevent him from being conceited)

Meditate on 2 Cor. 12:9-10

1. How are your weaknesses holding you back from
completing God's purpose for you?

2. How is your pride from education and experience preventing
you from depending on the Holy Spirit?

II. The Holy Spirit transforms believers.

John 3:5-6 (the Spirit gives new birth believers), John 16:8 (the
Spirit reveals sin), Rom. 8:5 (those who live according to the Spirit
set their minds on things of the Spirit and not the flesh), Gal. 5:17
(the desires of the Spirit are against the flesh), **Gal. 5:22-23 (the
Spirit produces God's fruit in you),** Rom. 7:6 (you have been
released from the law and live in the new way of the Spirit)

Meditate on Gal. 5:22-23

1. How is the Holy Spirit producing God's character in you?

2. What is preventing you from experiencing abundant fruit?

III. The Spirit teaches believers truth.

John 14:26 (Jesus told his disciples that the Spirit would teach
them all things and remind them of everything he said) John 16:13
(He will guide you in all truth), **1 Cor. 2:9-13 (The Spirit reveals
the truth),** Rom. 8:15-17 (the Spirit confirms your identity as a
child of God)

Meditate on 1 Cor. 2:9-12

1. How much are you depending on your own wisdom?

2. How do you try to play the role of the Holy Spirit in other people's lives?

IV. The Spirit guides believers in daily living.

John 14:16-18 (The Spirit is our Helper that lives with us and in us), Rom. 8:26-28 (the Spirit intercedes for believers according to the will of God), Rom. 8:14 (Believers are led by the Spirit), Ps. 139:7-10 (the Spirit leads and cares for believers)

Meditate on John 14:16-18

1.How frequently are you asking the Holy Spirit for guidance throughout the day?

V. The Spirit empowers believers for ministry.

Acts 1:8 (you will receive power when the Holy Spirit comes upon you), Acts 8:29 (the Spirit told Phillip to go to the Eunuch on the chariot)

Meditate on Acts 1:8

1. How dependent are you on programs and ministry activities?

5.2

CHURCH PLANTING

The purpose of missions is the expansion of the kingdom of God. Jesus did not explicitly command his disciples to plant churches, but he did command them to make disciples, baptize them and teach them to observe his commandments. These are all done within a community of believers known as the church.

> And Jesus came and said to them, "All authority on heaven and on earth has been given to me. Go therefore and make disciples of all nations, baptizing them in the name of the Father, and of the Son and of the Holy Spirit, teaching them to observe all that I have commanded you. And behold, I am with you always, to the end of the age" (Matt. 28:18-20).

Jesus intended the church to be a community of believers and not an institutionalized body. Missionaries can be intimidated by church planting as they confuse the church with an institutionalized building. Craig Ott explains that "the early church fathers often spoke of the church as the fellowship of the saints. Emphasis was rightly placed on the church as a people rather than as an institution."[32] *Ekklesia* is simply the assembly of God's people.

1. How has your idea of church planting been influenced by the Western institutionalized model?

What is the function of the church?

Acts is a historical narrative, and while Luke did not intend to set forth a specific model for the church, he did have certain motives for recording the early church history. Acts record the functions of the early church and the influence of the Holy Spirit.

> And they devoted themselves to the apostles' teaching and the fellowship, to the breaking of bread and the prayers. And awe came upon every soul, and many wonders and signs were being done through the apostles. And all who believed were together and had all things in common. And they were selling their possessions and belongings and distributing the proceeds to all, as any had need. And day by day, attending the temple together and breaking bread in their homes, they received their food with glad and sincere hearts, praising God and having favor with all people. And the Lord added to their number day by day those who were being saved (Acts 2:42-47).

From the teachings of Jesus and the example of the early church, it can be deduced that the core functions of the church are evangelism, gospel-centered teaching, baptism, fellowship,

---

[32] Craig Ott and Gene Wilson, *Global Church Planting: Biblical Principles and Best Practices for Multiplication,* (Grand Rapids: MI: Baker Academic, 2011) 5.

breaking of bread, prayer, serving one another and others in need, and praising God.

Duvall and Hays added, "The book of Acts shows us and tells us how God worked through the early church to change the world."[33] The Holy Spirit works through the church to accomplish God's will. When reading through Acts, readers are made very aware that God is in complete control and that his will and his sovereign plan are being accomplished through the church.

The church functions as the body of Christ, and each part fulfills a different function.

> For just as the body is one and has many members, and all the members of the body, though many, are one body, so it is with Christ. For in one Spirit, we were all baptized into one body, Jews or Greeks, slaves or free-and, all were made to drink of one Spirit (1 Cor. 12:12-13).

God gives each member of the body abilities to fulfill their role, but they are still completely dependent on the power of the Holy Spirit and not on their abilities. God requires obedience first, and then he equips the believer to fulfill his role.

1. What other functions of the church could be added?

2. How has the belief that you are not equipped delayed your service in the body?

---

[33] J. Scott Duvall and J. Daniel Hays, *Grasping God's Word* (Grand Rapids: Zondervan, 2012), 291.

What is church planting?

The church is not the kingdom of God but kingdom communities within the kingdom. In order to expand the kingdom of God, churches need to reproduce and multiply. Craig Ott defines church planting as "that ministry which through evangelism and discipleship establishes reproducing kingdom communities of believers in Jesus Christ who are committed to fulfilling biblical purposes under local spiritual leaders."[34] Healthy churches reproduce under spiritual leaders, but it is not required that those leaders are professional or seminary graduates. This is particularly true in unreached communities and house churches.

New church plants can be considered as competition and accused of sheep stealing, but they can revitalize communities. Tim Keller believes that planting new churches is the most important strategy for reaching a city[35]. Keller argues that new churches bring revitalized energy to a city. Churches that have existed for many years become stagnant and insider-focused, particularly if they become comfortable and reach a desirable size in the congregation. New churches are intentional in reaching outsiders as they desire to grow the church. While revitalizing a

---

[34] Ott and Wilson, *Global Church Planting, 7.*

[35] Tim Keller, "Cities and Salt", *Perspectives on the World Christian Movement*, (Pasadena: William Carey Library, 2009), 619.

city is important, there is a greater need for church planters around the world, especially within unreached people groups.

1. Why has church planting been perceived as something that can only be done by professionals?

2. What are some effective church planting methods that can be done by lay pastors with few resources?

God is a Missionary God

Since the fall, God has been working to restore his people back to himself. In Genesis 12:3, God promised Abraham that all peoples of the earth would be blessed through him. John Stott commented that it is God's plain purpose to take the gospel out to all families of the earth[36]. God's plan began with the nation of Israel. From the nation of Israel, the prophesied Messiah came as a Savior, not only for the Jews but all people.

1. How is God using the church to bring the nations back to him?

Cross-Cultural Church Planting

Paul began his ministry to the nations by preaching to the Jews and Gentiles, and it is the responsibility of all believers to continue his work in taking the name of Jesus to all nations. They will only

---

[36] John R.W Stott, "The Living God is a Missionary God", *Perspectives on the World Christian Movement*, (Pasadena: William Carey Library, 2009), 9.

be blessed when they hear and believe in the name of Jesus. Paul's teaching confirms the need to take the gospel out to all nations.

> How, then, can they call on the one they have not believed in? And how can they believe in the one whom they have not heard? And how can they hear without someone preaching to them? And how can anyone preach unless they are sent? As it is written: "How beautiful are the feet of those who bring good news!" (Romans 10:14-16).

Paul's priority on his missionary journeys was to preach the Gospel and plant churches where people had not heard of the life, death, and resurrection of Jesus.

1. What role should church planting have in missions?

The Task of Missions

Missions exist to make God known, and as discussed, this is done through kingdom communities of the church. John Piper elaborated, "Missions is not the ultimate goal of the church; worship is. Missions exist because worship doesn't."[37] The goal of missions is the glory of God and the expansion of the kingdom of God. Ott defined the task of mission "as the creation and expansion of kingdom communities among all the peoples of the earth to the glory of God."[38] Missions is a temporary task until all peoples of

---

[37] John Piper, *Let the Nations be Glad,* (Grand Rapids: MI: Baker Academic, 2010).

[38] Ott and Wilson, *Global Church Planting, 27.*

the earth have heard the name of Jesus and bow down before him at the final judgment.

1.What is your role in making God known and bringing glory to him?

5.3

THE MISSIONARY CHURCH

"The Church is by nature missionary to the extent that, if it ceases to be missionary, it has not just failed in one of its tasks, it has ceased to be the Church. Thus, the Church's self-understanding and sense of identity (its ecclesiology) is inherently bound up with its call to share and live out the Gospel of Jesus Christ to the ends of the earth and the end of time" (Kirk 2000, 31).[39]

Reflection and Discussion

1.Do you agree that a church without mission ceases to be the church? Explain your answer.

2. How would you describe the self-understanding of your church in relation to mission?

---

[39] Craig Ott and Stephen Strauss, *Encountering Theology of Mission*. (Grand Rapids, MI: Baker, 2010) 193.

CONCLUSION

As Jesus instructed his disciples, the need for disciple-makers is urgent. Biblical theology, understanding cultural differences, contextualization, preparing for culture shock, and planting churches are essential to cross-cultural discipleship. Most important is the heart's transformation for the disciple and disciple-maker.

Every disciple of Jesus has three options. Go, send, or disobey. If you are being called to go, discuss it with your pastor and begin researching sending agencies who will advise you further. You can also contact us at info@refugioministries.org or visit us at https://www.refugioministries.org/ for coaching and help along the way.

If you are being called to stay and support missionaries, speak to your church and find ways that you can help your missionaries financially, emotionally, and spiritually. Every missionary needs a strong support team from home. We offer workshops and coaching and would be honored to journey with you.

ABOUT REFUGIO MINISTRIES

Shaun and Stephanie began serving in ministry cross-culturally in 2007, and in 2015, they moved their family to southern Spain to serve a local church in the community. After a painful experience with that church, they began a new ministry work in town, planted two home churches, and began serving Spaniards, the international community, and college students in the city of Seville. Over the last 15 years, they have become friends with dozens of cross-cultural workers, ex-pats, and their families. They have become a trusted resource and referral for counseling and support for these

71

ex-pats and cross-cultural workers. This ministry was started to provide structured services of counseling, training, consulting, and writing support to cross-cultural workers worldwide. Get access to more resources, including free assessments and cross-cultural courses, at refugiministries.org.

BIBLIOGRAPHY

Bailey, Garrick and James Peoples. *Essentials of Cultural Anthropology*. Belmont, CA: Wadsworth/Cengage Learning, 2014.

Bock, Darrell. *Baker Exegetical Commentary on the New Testament: Acts*. Grand Rapids, MI: Baker Academic, 2007.

Bredfeldt, Gary J, and Lawrence O. Richards. *Creative Bible Teaching*. Chicago: Moody Publishers, 1998.

Carter, Terry G, J. Scott Duval, and J. Daniel Hays. *Preaching God's Word*. Grand Rapids, MI: Zondervan, 2005.

Chan, Sam. 2018. "GETTING OUR ACCENT RIGHT: Recognizing and Making the Most of an Enculturated Gospel." Christianity Today 62 (5): 50–56. https://search-ebscohost-com.ezproxy.liberty.edu/login.aspx?direct=true&db=lsdar&AN=ATLAiE58180528001124&site=ehost-live&scope=site.

Chester, Tim and Steve Timmis. *Total Church*. Wheaton, IL: Crossway, 2008.

Duvall, Scott J, and J. Daniel Hays. *Grasping God's Word*. Grand Rapids: Zondervan, 2012.

Elmer, Duane H. *Cross-Cultural Connections: Stepping Out and Fitting in Around the World*. Downers Grove, IL: Intervarsity Press, 2002.

Fee, Gordon, D and Douglas Stuart. *How to Read the Bible for All Its Worth. Grand Rapids: Zondervan, 2003*.

Goldsworthy, Graeme. *According to Plan*. Intervarsity Press, 2009.

Hamilton, James M. Jr. *What is Biblical Theology?* Wheaton, IL: Crossway, 2014.

Hiebert, Paul G. *The Gospel in Human Contexts: Anthropological Explorations for Contemporary Missions*. Grand Rapids, MI: Baker Academic, 2009.

Howell, Brian M., Paris, Jenell. Introducing Cultural Anthropology: A Christian Perspective. United States: Baker Publishing Group, (n.d.).

Joannes, David. *The mind of a Missionary: What Global Kingdom Workers Tell Us About Thriving on Mission Today*. Within Reach Global Inc., 2018.

Keller, Tim. "Cities and Salt." *Perspectives on the World Christian Movement*. Pasadena: William Carey Library, 2009.

Livermore, David A. *Leading with cultural intelligence the real secret to success*. New York, NY: American Management Association, 2015.

McKnight, Scot, Dallas Willard, and N. T. Wright. *The King Jesus Gospel: The Original Good News Revisited*. Grand Rapids, MI: Zondervan, 2016.

Ott, Craig and Stephen Strauss. *Encountering Theology of Mission*. Grand Rapids, MI: Baker Academic, 2010.

Ott, Criag and Gene Wilson. *Global Church Planting: Biblical Principles and Best Practices for Multiplication*. Grand Rapids: MI: Baker Academic, 2011.

Oberg, Kalvero. "Culture Shock: Adjustment to New Cultural Environments," Practical Anthropology 7, no. 4 (1967): 177.

Parshall, Phil, "Going Too Far?" *Perspectives on the World Christian Movement*. 4th ed. Pasadena, CA: William Carey, 2009.

Piper, John. *Let the Nations be Glad*. Grand Rapids: MI: Baker Academic, 2010.

Platt, David. *Radical*. Colorado Springs: Multnomah Books, 2010.

Stott, John R.W. "The Living God is a Missionary God." *Perspectives on the World Christian Movement*. Pasadena: William Carey Library, 2009.

Terry, John M and Robert L. Gallagher, *Encountering the History of Missions: From the Early Church to Today*, (Grand Rapids, MI: Baker, 2017.

Ting-Toomey, Stella and Leeva C. Chung. *Understanding Intercultural Communication*. Oxford, NY: Oxford University Press, 2012.

Travis, John J. "Appropriate Approaches in Muslim Contexts." *Appropriate Christianity*. CA: William Carey, 2005.

Travis, John J. "Must all Muslims Leave Islam to Follow Jesus?" *Perspectives on the World Christian Movement*. 4th ed. Pasadena, CA: William Carey, 2009.

Printed in Great Britain
by Amazon

45202226R00046